HOPSCOTCH
STORIES OF

The

Great Night Journey

First published in 2009 by
Franklin Watts
338 Euston Road
London
NW1 3BH

Franklin Watts Australia
Level 17/207 Kent Street
Sydney
NSW 2000

A CIP catalogue record for this book is available
from the British Library.

ISBN 978 0 7496 8372 6 (hbk)
ISBN 978 0 7496 8378 8 (pbk)

Series Editor: Melanie Palmer
Series Advisor: Dr Barrie Wade
Series Designer: Peter Scoulding
Consultant: Professor Ghulam Sarwar

Printed in China

Franklin Watts is a division of
Hachette Children's Books,
an Hachette Livre UK company.
www.hachettelivre.co.uk

STORIES OF RELIGION

The
Great Night
Journey

by Anita Ganeri and Emma Garner

FRANKLIN WATTS
LONDON•SYDNEY

About this book

The story of the Great Night Journey comes from the religion of Islam. Islam began in the Middle East some 1,400 years ago. Muslims (followers of Islam) believe that Allah (God) sent a series of prophets to teach people how to live. The last and greatest of these was Muhammad (Peace Be Upon Him*). Muhammad (PBUH) was born in the city of Makkah in Arabia (modern-day Saudi Arabia) in about 570 CE. *The Great Night Journey* tells how Allah gave Muhammad the instructions that Muslims should say their prayers five times each day.

* This is abbreviated to PBUH after the first mention. Following Islamic tradition, the illustrations in this book do not show faces of people or depictions of Allah or Muhammad (PBUH).

Long ago, the Prophet Muhammad
(Peace Be Upon Him) was living
in the city of Makkah.

One night, the Prophet was sleeping in his house when he was woken up by the angel Jibril.

The angel told Muhammad (PBUH) that he had come to take him on an amazing journey.

He showed Muhammad (PBUH)
an animal that looked like a small
white horse for him to ride on.
Its name was Buraq, or Lightning.

Then, in a flash, they sped through the skies until they reached the city of Jerusalem.

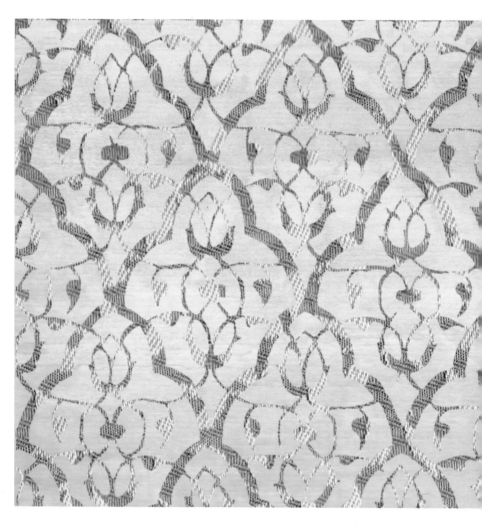

The angel Jibril led Muhammad (PBUH) to the Gate of the Keepers, the first gate of heaven.

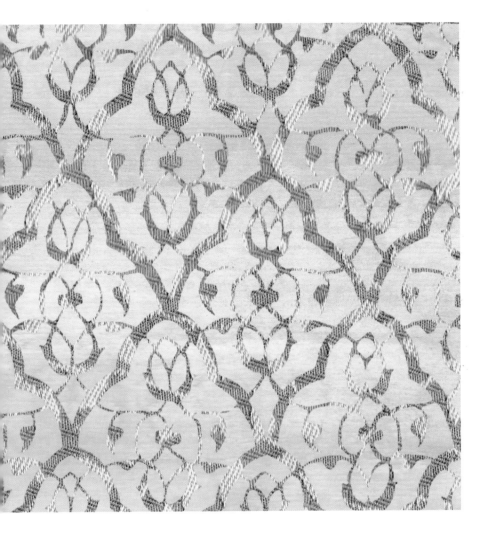

"Is he the Prophet?" a voice asked.

"Yes, it's him" Jibril replied.

"Bring him to me," said the voice.

So Jibril led Muhammad (PBUH)
through the gate, and all the way
up through the seven heavens.

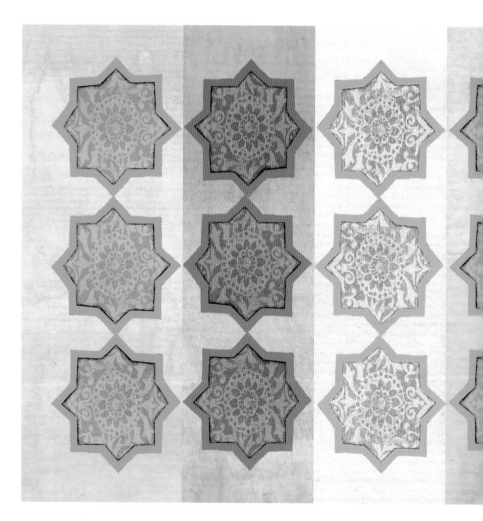

In each of the seven heavens, Muhammad (PBUH) met the prophets that had come before him.

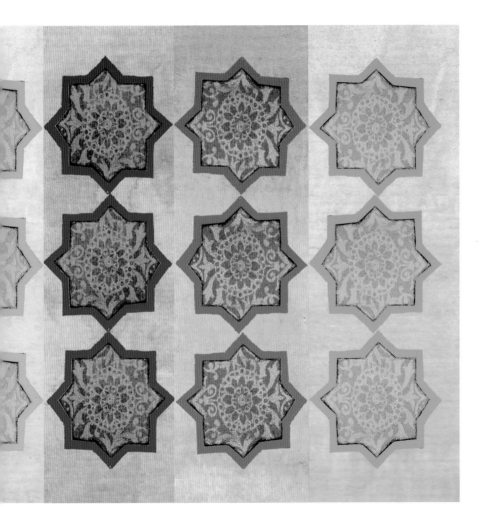

At last, Muhammad (PBUH) and Jibril reached the gate of the seventh heaven.

"You are welcome," said the voice. Muhammad (PBUH) knew it was the voice of Allah.

Muhammad (PBUH) was given three goblets: one with wine, one with milk and the third with honey. He had to choose one.

He took the goblet of milk and drank it. He knew Muslims must not drink wine.

Then, in the highest heaven,
Muhammad (PBUH) was given
Allah's command.

Allah told Muhammad (PBUH)
that Muslims should say their
prayers fifty times each day.

19

On his way back to earth to give his people the news, Muhammad (PBUH) met the Prophet Musa.

"What has Allah ordered?" asked Musa. Muhammad (PBUH) replied, "To pray fifty times each day."

"But that is too much," said Musa. "People will not be able to say that many prayers every day."

"Go back to Allah and ask him to make it less. Then people will obey his command."

So Muhammad (PBUH) went back up to the seventh heaven, and Allah agreed to make it ten fewer prayers each day.

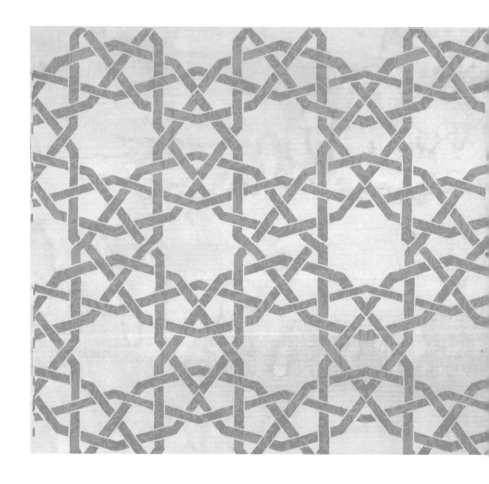

But when Muhammad (PBUH) came back and told Musa, Musa said that this was still too much.

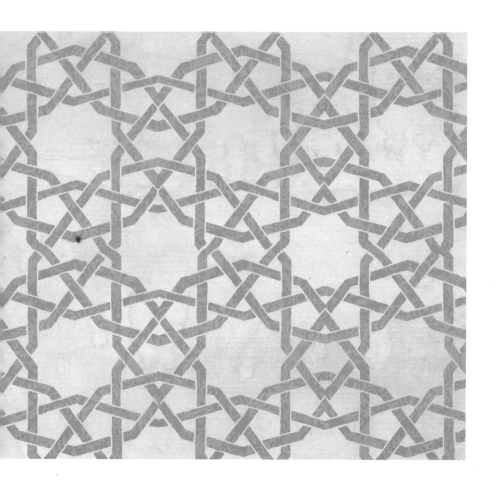

Muhammad went up and down
from Allah to Musa until it was
just five prayers each day.

"Praying five times a day will
bring the same reward as five
hundred prayers," said Musa.

Now he had Allah's command,
Muhammad (PBUH) had to return
to Makkah before the sun rose.

He climbed onto Buraq's back and raced, lightning fast, through the skies with his news.

This is why Muslims today pray five times each day – at dawn, midday, mid-afternoon, sunset and just before bedtime.

When they pray, they face towards the holy city of Makkah, where the Prophet Muhammad (PBUH) was born.

Hopscotch has been specially designed to fit the requirements of the Literacy Framework. It offers real books by top authors and illustrators for children developing their reading skills.

For more details go to:
www.franklinwatts.co.uk

* hardback